COUNTRY

Style & Design

COUNTRY
Style & Design

JUSTIN BISHOP

images
Publishing

Published in Australia in 2012 by
The Images Publishing Group Pty Ltd
ABN 89 059 734 431
6 Bastow Place, Mulgrave, Victoria 3170, Australia
Tel: +61 3 9561 5544 Fax: +61 3 9561 4860
books@imagespublishing.com
www.imagespublishing.com

Copyright © The Images Publishing Group Pty Ltd 2012
The Images Publishing Group Reference Number: 977

National Library of Australia Cataloguing-in-Publication entry:

Author:	Bishop, Justin.
Title:	Country Style & Design / Justin Bishop
ISBN:	9781864704488 (hbk.)
Subjects:	Country homes—Decoration. Interior decoration.
Other Authors/Contributors:	Ball, Debbie.
Dewey Number:	747

Edited by Debbie Ball

Designed by The Graphic Image Studio Pty Ltd, Mulgrave,
Australia
www.tgis.com.au

Pre-publishing services by United Graphic Pte Ltd, Singapore

Printed by Everbest Printing Co. Ltd., in Hong Kong/China on
150 gsm Quatro Silk Matt paper

IMAGES has included on its website a page for special notices
in relation to this and our other publications. Please visit
www.imagespublishing.com

For further information contact Justin Bishop at
www.justinbishop.com.au

Contents

Profile

Justin Bishop is passionate about timeless country interior design, traditional design and decoration. His personal design principles echo an age of well-loved enduring classics and comforting time-honoured style.

He was raised at historic 'Pigeon Bank', his family's ancestral home in Melbourne's tranquil Yarra Valley, where he joined his family in the delicate restoration of the property. During his childhood and formative years Justin developed an innate sense of period style and traditional craftsmanship from being involved in the restoration at Pigeon Bank; skills he would later demonstrate when creating his first range of decorative architectural miniatures. He studied graphic design, theatre design and fine art, however it was the 'hands on' approach to design he developed at Pigeon Bank that affected and inspired him the most.

This approach, together with his passion for classical architecture, was to form the core of Justin's business endeavours. In January 2001, Justin opened his first workshop and showroom in Richmond, Victoria where he produced a wide range of decorative interior design products. Extensive travel overseas during this time provided great inspiration for his work and clients throughout Australia, Europe and the United States have since commissioned items from his collections. Justin has been a regular exhibitor at home and garden shows nationally, such as The Australian National Trusts Heritage and Restoration Show and Melbourne's RACV Home Show.

Justin's passion for traditional design is also evident in his interior design style, where his training at Melbourne's Swinburne University has been combined with the skills he developed over his lifetime. Known for his sophisticated blend of well-loved vintage furniture and classic interior items, Justin's work has appeared in a variety of leading magazines and interior publications, including *Australian Country Style*, *The Age* newspaper and the *British House* magazine.

In July 2006, Justin purchased an original cottage in the picturesque town of Sassafras in Melbourne's Dandenong Ranges. The property was time-worn and sadly neglected yet Justin was instantly drawn to the property's charm and he is currently restoring the house and garden to their original condition. Filled with his selection of vintage furniture and collectables, the house will undoubtedly become a masterpiece of Justin Bishop's classic signature style of 'country'.

Introduction

If I claimed to be an authority on any particular interior design style, it would be the style that is 'country'.

From my grassroots, growing up in my family's ancestral home in Melbourne's Yarra Valley, to travelling through rural areas in countries all around the world, the simple, pared-down classic style of country has long been engrained in my psyche.

For many years I have had a desire to produce a book. I knew it would happen when the time was right; when I felt I had something to say, something worthy of putting down on paper. It became clear over time that a book featuring beautiful country interiors, exteriors and gardens would be a perfect vehicle for my knowledge, experience and design ethic. Based on traditional country style with clean, modern influences, the book would be a collection of inspirational images, style notes and stories that represent the essence of 'country interior design' as I know it.

I have stayed
true to my
belief that
style is simple;
it should only be what it needs to
be, nothing more and nothing less.

I decided to travel and research, write and photograph. To discover visions, places, stories and things that represent the country style that I know and love. My idea was to present a stunning book for those wishing to emulate this style of design; whether they live in the country or the city, in a mansion or an apartment. They may be relocating, renovating, or simply looking to be taken on a journey by a book about a style that they love.

My style has always been classic, void of colour and decorative trends. I have stayed true to my belief that style is simple; it should only be what it needs to be, nothing more and nothing less. The style of my parents and indeed my rural upbringing has curbed my approach to design and it's this approach that appears throughout this book.

I have presented this book as a 'collection' that will inform, entertain and inspire its readers. Not a typical country book, but a representation of *my* vision of what is 'country style and design'.

My style has always been classic,
void of colour and decorative trends.

My Country Life

I began collecting years, old furniture; interesting objects; all

My interior design ambitions began as a boy. Growing up in rural Victoria in my family's ancestral property 'Pigeon Bank', was a magical experience. My parents allowed my passion for creativity to run wild as we spent years renovating the property.

My bedroom was my proudest achievement, with restored floorboards, white-washed tongue-and-groove lining boards (reaching to 13-foot ceilings) and antique fittings. It was a large room and I used old ship sails to divide areas, draping them theatrically, yet simply. I began collecting during these early years, old furniture; cushions; and interesting objects; all of which told a story. I would create displays and photograph them (when I was lucky enough to borrow my parents' camera).

My parents bought historic Pigeon Bank in the late 1970s. Originally a 180-acre property, it belonged to my mother's great grandparents who built the majority of the home in 1886. The large Victorian homestead, perched high on a hill in Kangaroo

during these early cushions; and of which told a story.

Ground, is in the southern tip of Australia's Great Dividing Range and commands views of Melbourne and beyond.

My great-great-grandfather, a member of Victorian parliament, ran the property as a prize-winning farm breeding Clydesdale horses. He, his wife and 11 children lived at Pigeon Bank until his death in 1915 when the house and its contents were sold out of the family. Changing hands several times, the house and gardens underwent many style incarnations, from neat 1920's chic to 1960's modernism. By the time we took over the reins it was quite a collection of styles.

My parents' vision was clear: to restore the property to its original condition with genuine period details. My father was keen to give the house a grand facelift. Sometimes his decision-making leant more towards 'City Mansion' than 'Country Farmhouse', however my mother held her ground firmly. The renovation and restoration of Pigeon Bank was sympathetic to its origins and it personified true country style.

I spent many weekends in the back seat of my parents' car travelling around Melbourne on a quest as we began a new room.

During my childhood, there was constant activity at home; we moved our living spaces around the house as we tackled the restoration of various sections one at a time. Twentieth-century additions were removed or transformed as we uncovered many original fittings and fixtures that were promptly restored and returned to their former glory. Details were researched with the help of local craftsmen and by scouring notes and photographs of our family history, as the house was returned to its Victorian splendour.

I was always excited by our next project. It meant trips into town to visit restoration hardware stores and clearance yards searching for materials. I spent many weekends in the back seat of my parents' car travelling around Melbourne on a quest as we began a new room. Every weekend saw a new challenge as we set out to strip back original architectural fittings, doors and architraves to their original condition or to choose colours to match a tiny sample of something original we found on a wall, under layers of wallpaper and paint.

As the restoration progressed, stepping into the property became like stepping back in time. An authentic sense of history filled the rooms. The presence of our ancestors was always felt, as their photographs and belongings were often proudly on display. All furniture and accessories were true to the origins of the house and any modern conveniences were hidden or concealed behind period details.

I valued our magical lifestyle immensely and loved being part of it. My first bedroom in the house was quite plain, in true Victorian farmhouse style. I began collecting old bits and pieces to add interest and to play my role in the recreation of the property's period style. I remember once asking for an antique toy fire engine for my birthday rather than something modern, as my school friends would have no doubt preferred.

While we worked on the house, the grounds at Pigeon Bank were also transformed and again, we salvaged all we could of the original property. Time-worn farm fences were restored, outbuildings rebuilt, and gardens replanted with the help of family photos and some fading memories of elderly relatives who had known the property in its heyday.

Here, we added our own additions: building country sheds in Victorian style including an enormous two-storey barn with stable doors and an attic. We also extended the gardens. After restoring the original house surrounds with Victorian specimens and traditional layouts, we added a further five acres of landscaping, which included garden rooms and open lawns bordered with hedges, a croquet lawn with its own pavilion and a large ornamental lake complete with jetty and an island.

I did not know it then, but looking back
an amazing gift it was to be a part

now, I realise what of my parents' journey.

We always kept an array of livestock including horses, Hereford cattle, sheep and poultry; all housed in well-designed period style stables and well-fenced yards. Walking through the farm's many open paddocks on my way to school each morning was always an adventure.

At home, as a family, we worked together on many projects. At first I was a quiet observer and as I grew, I became very 'hands on', designing and constructing new additions alongside my parents. I did not know it then, but looking back now, I realise what an amazing gift it was to be a part of my parents' journey.

Not only was I able to watch them refine and master many practical and creative skills, but I also saw their passion for the creative process. It rubbed off on me and has stayed with me ever since.

Style

My Thoughts on Style

Style in 'country' design will always be interpreted in many different ways. A person's place of birth and life experiences can determine their view on the subject. Its perception can differ within landscape, language, culture, religious beliefs and the various arts and crafts movements of the past.

Even to the untrained eye, there seems to be a common thread that comes through this design genre. 'True' country style usually exudes an *authentic* quality. Raw materials, natural and unaffected, are often handcrafted and transformed into useful objects, furnishings and architecture. It is a wholesome, genuine approach to design that remains simple, practical and uncomplicated.

Rarely are country-inspired homes uptight or uncomfortable, since they share the common ideal that the main purpose of a 'country' space is to create a liveable, welcoming and relaxed environment.

I have been lucky enough to travel through many different parts of the world and have seen many different styles of country design; from grand homesteads on cattle stations in outback Australia; to the simple teak dwellings in mountain villages of Southeast Asia; to rustic ranch houses and barns in open, green landscapes of upstate New York.

Therefore my take on the subject is a blend of my own background mixed with many other styles that I have seen and this melting pot of styles has given me an overall belief about what is 'country'.

Traditionally, country style harks back to an era that appears quieter when viewed from today's world. A time before modern machine technology and mass production; a time when function came before form; and form held a graceful simplicity and an elegant charm, as well as being predominantly useful.

A time before
technology and mass
when function came

I often see timber, metal, glass and porcelain as solid natural materials with a sturdy, no-fuss attitude. My own ancestors lived a comfortable life in the country. Their world was filled with practical objects that were tough enough to stand the test of time, as well as being well designed and aesthetically pleasing.

Country style becomes a way of life for many people. They embrace an understanding and appreciation of a wholesome standard of living that embodies the uncomplicated and an essence of freshness. Country aesthetics support a manner of doing and being, such as social interaction, enjoyment and often a hard-working yet relaxed existence.

modern machine production; a time before form ...

Country style becomes a way of life for many people.

For me, country style interior design has a comfortable, lived-in look that promotes welcoming, social spaces. It is casually elegant with a complement of sturdy, practical furniture, natural textiles, with a mix of useful and whimsical accents. Exterior elements are equally as practical and designed with a hardworking lifestyle in mind to survive natural elements and often harsh conditions, and it also emanates a natural and effortless charm.

The country design styles that I most admire are those of America, France, England and Australia. These countries approach their design with a relaxed, purposeful, yet simple attitude. They stay true to their historical roots, remaining largely unaffected by modern trends, which results in a confidence that comes through in each style.

Country interior design is a compilation of all of these styles, rather than an exact representation of each distinct style on its own. The different styles of outback Australia, the French country style of Provence, the floral English country style; and rustic Americana blend in an eclectic fashion, to create a fresh approach to country interior design. We will, however begin our journey with an analysis of each style prior to successfully merging them together.

All the styles and their elements allow us to traverse into the creative process where a successful meld of these styles will form 'country interior design'.

English Country Style

'English' country style is elegant and traditional. It is a blend of classic farmhouse style furnishings mixed with a slightly aged country estate look. It creates a romantic environment full of decorative styling, with an emphasis on over-accessorising and clutter.

In an English country room, I love to accessorise with rows of leather books and collections of classic items, such as top hats and walking sticks, bronze statues and historic portraits. Images of horses and hounds, classic hunting scenes and country gentry are my personal favourites here.

The furniture is reminiscent of an old English country estate and often includes large wooden bookcases and other handmade

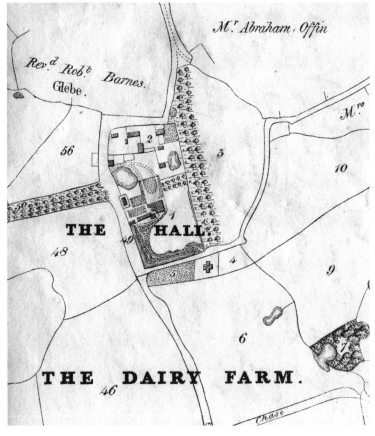

English country emphasises the functionality of furniture.

pieces in deep walnut or mahogany. Tables, dressers and desks are typically made of oak, mahogany or pine. Accents, such as the metalwork on furniture, doors and windows are often made of brass and show signs of age. Sofas and chairs tend to be deep-seated and upholstered with richly patterned fabrics. Throw pillows or upholstered pads soften the look and feel of wooden chairs and window seats. English country emphasises the functionality of furniture and pieces tend to be well worn, yet considerably sturdy.

Whether the home is a small cottage or sprawling estate, English country style should project a traditional elegance that is relaxed and comfortable. It often features floral and other natural elements and the colours reflect the hues of nature. English country style is a way of bringing an English garden indoors. It is naturally

casual and unceremonious, yet if you accessorise correctly, you can bring a touch of formality to it.

The colour palette in English country style can be dark and almost foreboding, using a lot of deep red, brown and faded antique colours. Aged leather, plaid and tweed are commonly used textiles, although floral fabrics and fine delicate prints also have their place.

English country decorating often features an abundance of well-crafted period details, such as beamed ceilings, wainscoting and wood floors. Vases filled with fresh flowers from the garden or baskets of dried flowers are scattered throughout the home. English country style should not look planned or designed, but rather the result of generations living in a home.

Images of horses and hounds, and classic hunting scenes, are my personal favourites.

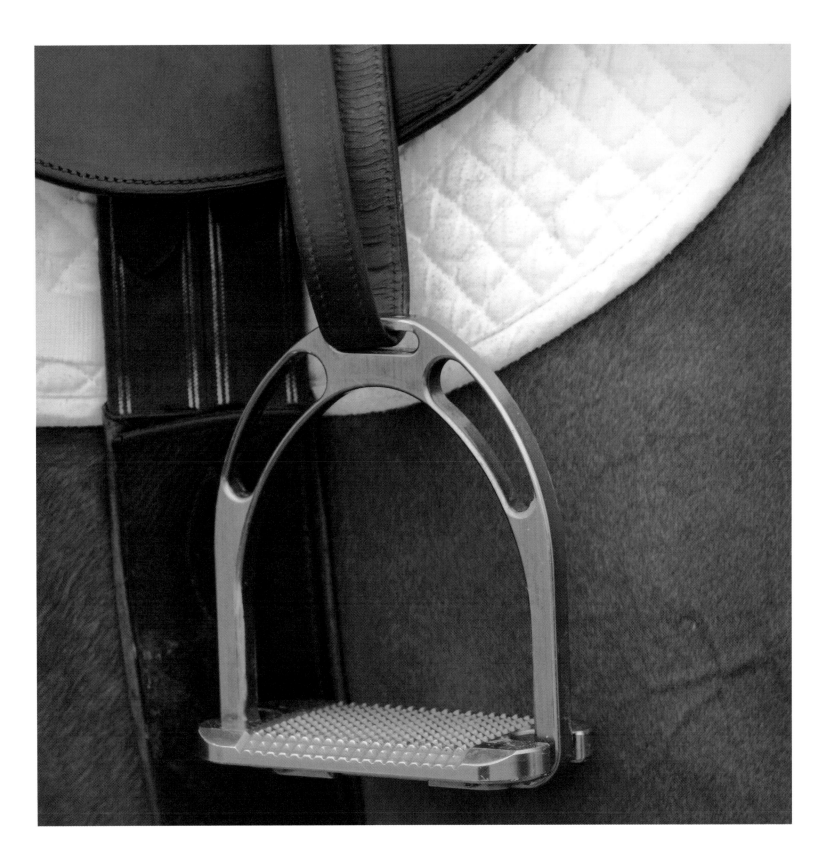

French Country Style

'French' country style is known for its relaxed glamour teamed with subtle elegance. The atmosphere of a home furnished and accessorised with French country decor is effortlessly chic without structure or harsh formality.

Graceful and light, it is known for its use of subtle, pale colours mixed with natural materials, giving it a slightly raw yet sophisticated look. French country style combines a simple and practical approach to decorating, while sustaining a well put together, glamorous edge.

The style of French country design that I love is unpretentious and natural. Colours include soft blues and pale reds, pale creamy yellows, natural greens and earthy tones. Decorative items are often made of iron, copper and brass, wood and stone. Lightly weathered timber accessories blended with hand-forged iron details and creamy white ceramics are common.

Furniture is sturdy and basic, often handmade in pine and oak. Classic French country furniture includes large plank-style dining tables surrounded by ladder-back dining chairs or benches, large, carved armoires and four-poster beds. When furnishing a room in French country style, I try to include furniture with hand-carved timber detailing and soft delicate shapes. Sofas and chairs with rustic upholstery and timber furniture pieces that have been antiqued or coated with a French wash are my personal favourites.

The style of French country design

unpretentious and

that I love is natural. Decorative items are often made of iron, copper, brass, wood and stone.

Fabrics are also simple and natural, usually with a small floral or a fine stripe. Toile is a traditional French country fabric. A white, cream or yellow background can feature large 'country' motifs in a single contrasting colour, such as black, blue, red, or green. Accessories, including vintage kitchenware and other practical household items, are often handmade.

An important element in pieces used in French country style decorating is the use of natural, earthy materials. Timber dining chairs and footstools with woven rush seating are a typical example here. Architecturally, natural stone fireplaces, wooden floors, rough-stained or painted plaster walls and hefty beamed ceilings give texture and simplicity to the look.

Pale weathered timber accessories blended with hand-forged iron details and creamy white ceramics are common.

American Country Style

'American' country style is about more than just decorating a home. It is about American history, the country's forefathers and the vast open lands that they pioneered.

American country furniture is practical, as well as decorative. Strong masculine lines work best: leather chairs and sofas, large round wooden dining tables and handmade cabinetry complement this style perfectly. As always, the accessories are all important, with Native American blankets in muted colours, hide or skin rugs and throws and antlers.

American history plays a major part in home furnishings and decorations of American country style. Pioneers on their wagon trails used materials at hand and wood was a major influence

American country style ranges from the rugged log cabins of the mountain areas to the refined country cottages by the coast.

from early pioneer days, used in both furniture and home construction. The wood was often white-washed or left unpainted and unfinished in order for the natural wood grain to complement the historic style.

It is about rustic architecture and furnishings and its signature look is branded by handcrafted architectural detailing including rough-cut log framework, large open-plan rooms, stone fireplaces and wide-plank floors.

Predominantly handmade, American country style ranges from the rugged log cabins of the mountain areas to the refined country cottages by the coast. American country architecture is earthy and simple, while retaining a strong sense of quality and grandeur. I try to make an American-style home feel polished and refined, while maintaining a certain rustic, 'handmade' edge.

American country style ... is about American history, the country's forefathers and the vast open lands that they pioneered.

Colour is everything when working with this type of decorating. The hues in American country styling are typically dark tones. Forest-green and various shades of brown played off against white-washed or natural timber walls, work well. Of course the red, white and blue of the American flag is a must. Aged and historic if possible, the patriotic star-spangled banner is a personal favourite; I include it wherever possible.

American country decor is unique to the United States. It says 'Americana', while keeping the traditions of what an American home looked like centuries ago. An American country home presents a sense of nostalgia and history, all the while embracing the occupants and visitors of the house with a personal and comfortable atmosphere.

Aged and historic the patriotic star-banner is a personal I include it wherever possible.

if possible,

spangled

favourite;

Australian Country Style

'Australian' country style differs from other country styles, in that it is relatively new; however, it is a perfect example of pure and simple styling and, I think, it is truly one of the best.

The style stems from the country's beginnings, when its early settlers pioneered its rugged landscape, with bare essentials. These settlers survived with the skills they brought with them, adapting these skills to cope with their new surroundings. On the whole, the style is plain and simple. Designs brought here from faraway lands were recreated, albeit in a plainer and less complicated manner.

The style stems from the country's beginnings, when its early settlers pioneered it with bare essentials.

Architecturally, the style was designed to cope with the country's often harsh conditions. Wide verandahs provided cool refuge from relentless heat in the outback. Stilt foundations raised living spaces above threatening floods in the tropical north. In the south, basic slab huts were built as protection from the cold, often with crude bush carpentry, which was later improved as skills were developed.

In the earliest days, basic materials sufficed when creating home decor. Old packaging from household supplies was put to good use. Hessian, newspapers and canvas were used to line walls and to creative decorative elements. Crates and storage boxes were fashioned into practical furniture pieces. Later, cedar, mahogany and pine were used to build more elaborate furnishings, often mimicking international styles, but in a slightly pared-down, simpler way.

Australian country style became a blend of these elements. With Europe, America and Asia influencing the mix, it evolved into a true melting pot of styles.

Colours reflected nature. Natural tones of white, stone, cream and ochre were popular with woody timber accents. For me, this plain 'non-colour' scheme is the essence of this look and one that I have embraced many times.

Natural tones of white, stone, cream, and ochre were popular with woody timber accents.

Design

My Thoughts
on Design

When I approach interior design in order to achieve a certain look, I must always be clear of the direction in which I am heading. Rather than mimicking other existing designs, I start the process with a clean slate, an open mind. Wherever possible, I try to create a new style. I start by finding inspiration. With country style for example, I might look at nature. I choose the colours, textures and forms that appeal to me. I collect images and create a visual diary noting the elements that reappear the most. A style starts to form.

The design process can then slowly proceed with a clear understanding of what is to be achieved. Elements from the images I have collected will begin to reappear as I start to design. The choices about architecture and interior space, through to colour, fabrics and the most detailed of furnishings can be made with the confidence that I am heading in a firm direction.

The end result will not only be harmonious, but will be a clear reflection of a well-defined style.

Designing a country home is about creating a warm and welcoming feeling where family members and friends can converge to spend time, feel relaxed and be comfortable. With antique elements and calming colours, I establish a casual environment that has a natural, rustic charm and innate timelessness.

Country style is rich in history and tradition and creates a place of warmth, belonging and an unpretentious lifestyle, such as my ancestors enjoyed. A country home should be designed with a practical and functional attitude combined with a simple decorative

aesthetic. It is an approach that has spanned decades and will serve as a standard for years to come.

In most instances, country-style furnishings should also be natural and antique. I try to use wooden pieces with rustic linen or cotton upholstery at every opportunity. Country-style furniture should evoke history and often has a story to tell. Older pieces with worn, painted surfaces, rustic hardware and handmade detailing are ideal for evoking the emotion as country design does. Many older pieces of furniture have painted finishes that have faded over time, revealing the wood's character and history that hides beneath the surface.

Wood, metal and natural fibres are prominent features in a country-themed home. Wicker is an essential component, often seen in basketware with a raw texture, used for informal storage. Hand-made items made from natural materials are ideal.

Antique homewares, such as household tools and kitchen utensils, genuinely captivate an admirer. I collect old wooden boxes; interior hardware; tin signs; toys; kitchen gadgets and other curiosities that can be displayed on shelves and tabletops or tucked away in a corner. For me, filling a room with vintage, well-loved items conveys an unmistakable feeling of comfort and belonging.

Wherever possible I cover floors in original tongue-and-groove floorboards. They are stained to reflect the colours of the stylistic design chosen. Rugs are also a decorative and practical accompaniment to a country room. A well-chosen rug will add style, as well as soften the hardness of a wooden floor.

Windows are an essential part of any decorating scheme and are often the finishing touch to a well-decorated room. Be sympathetic to the furnishings and period involved. Rather than being a feature, choose simple treatments that blend in with the overall design scheme.

The correct choice of fabrics is imperative. Delicate prints in a variety of soft colours definitely say 'country'. However, stripes and strong solids can find a place in many country interpretations. I often use classic red, white and blue – popular country accent colours – and add them using striped or bold solid fabrics. These fabrics work best when slightly faded and time-worn.

A traditional farmhouse kitchen is my favourite place to start when creating a country interior. I try to make practical and functional additions a priority. I fill old cupboards with sets of authentic vintage crockery, antique silverware, glass jars, cream china and copper pots. I source original hardware, such as aged brass or porcelain door handles and add it to the cabinetry. I install deep apron sinks in place of something modern and aluminium. I hunt down old rustic tables and use original kitchen linen to add style. What I enjoy most is the opportunity to wander through secondhand markets and antique shops to find the perfect additions. I look for vintage kitchen tools, crockery, glassware, cookbooks and fabrics.

Country

Try to use the same sense of style when designing other areas of a home. Country style decor should represent a time from the past and suggest a gentler pace of living. Rustic wooden furniture with hard-wearing natural cotton and linen fabrics, handcrafted antiques and family heirlooms are good examples of this. Original family items including photographs, handwritten letters and vintage clothing can be displayed to create collections of memorabilia. Country interior decorating should show a sense of history and tradition.

There are many variations within the theme of country. Sometimes I use vintage pieces from all over the world to build an international country look. This can be very effective when creating a more 'eclectic' style of country room. Items from different countries intentionally displayed to feature their culture and craftsmanship can add style and character, when done with care. An eclectic country style is often whimsical and slightly quirky; it should never be taken too seriously.

style is rich in history and tradition.

Of course, country style does not always have to be true to authenticity and history. If I am asked to work in a more contemporary style, I hunt for impressive vintage handmade pieces and display them in a modern 'gallery' format. I achieve this with simple, clean lines and furniture and items that are quite plain in style. With the correct treatment, a country look can be blended into many different styles of decorating.

Colour and Texture

When designing a country home, there is nothing I love more than a totally neutral colour scheme.

For me, a blend of natural textures teamed with a predominantly natural colour palette is timeless and pure. Aged timber furniture upholstered with coarsely woven linen, natural calico sitting amongst faded wicker basketware and antique brass combined with handmade natural tiles are perfect combinations.

Using natural elements to build the aesthetics of a room will almost always result in a timeless finish. There is nothing faddish about a basic natural colour scheme. It works particularly well when creating a country look, something that I have demonstrated in the pages of this book. Soft aged natural colours, without the interruption of complicated prints or bright colours, sit well with my design ethos.

I have often said that I do not like colour. For the most part, this is true. I do, however, use colour on the odd occasion as an accent or to work in with an existing scheme. The correct colour choice plays an important part in setting the tone for a country house and I use natural colours wherever possible. Colours that calm, such as white, beige, brown and antique gold work into the accents of a 'country' colour scheme. These colours are integrated on walls, found in floor coverings and divulged in decorative accents.

154

Wherever possible I like colour to be faded and aged; to have been painted or printed years ago and have lost its strength over time. While this may sound like a purely decorative concept, it works well in practical situations. It is as much about the colour itself as the objects that I combine. I might use faded blue linen on a kitchen breakfast table, red leather in a dining room study or soft green silk curtains on a window looking out to a garden.

A controlled use of colour will not overpower a room, but draw harmony into it. It is a subtle approach and works well when combined with an otherwise neutral colour palette.

Kitchen and Dining Room Design

My thoughts on a traditional country kitchen stem from my childhood. Our kitchen at home was simple and practical; it exuded perfect country style. It was a typical country kitchen built with rustic timber and original fittings. It had an open feel and it adjoined our breakfast room, which was designed in the same style.

A country kitchen should always be practical. Regularly used items can look great left out in the open, on shelving or hooks, rather than being hidden away in cupboards. The accessories that are placed throughout a room really emphasise a style and this certainly applies to the accessories in a country kitchen. A standard for me in a country kitchen is 'controlled clutter'. I always keep a selection of original kitchen tools and accessories out on display. If grouped correctly in vintage jugs or pots, they add to

A country

the charm of a country home. I allow pots and pans, glass jars with food, stacks of vintage crockery and cooking and eating utensils to become part of the decor. Food and supplies can also double as decorative accessories; red apples in a bowl, white eggs in a basket and fresh herbs in glass vases all add to an effortless country style.

When choosing furniture, built-in benches and cupboards are practical but I always insist on a few freestanding pieces as well. Original wooden dressers, side tables and chairs add to the feel of a country dining room. Where there is room, a large farmhouse table is a wonderful piece to have. It can be used for entertaining as well as providing extra bench space. An old china cabinet crammed with a collection of cream dishes, jugs, teacups and coordinated kitchen 'odds and ends' is another of my personal favourites.

kitchen should always be practical.

In most cases, I play with the design of tile-work and other architectural detailing but keep the finished look harmonious by using a mostly white-on-white colour scheme. This always looks fresh and is the perfect backdrop for a collection of vintage accessories.

A standard for me in a country kitchen is 'controlled clutter'.

In most cases, I
other architectural

168

play with the design of tile-work and detailing.

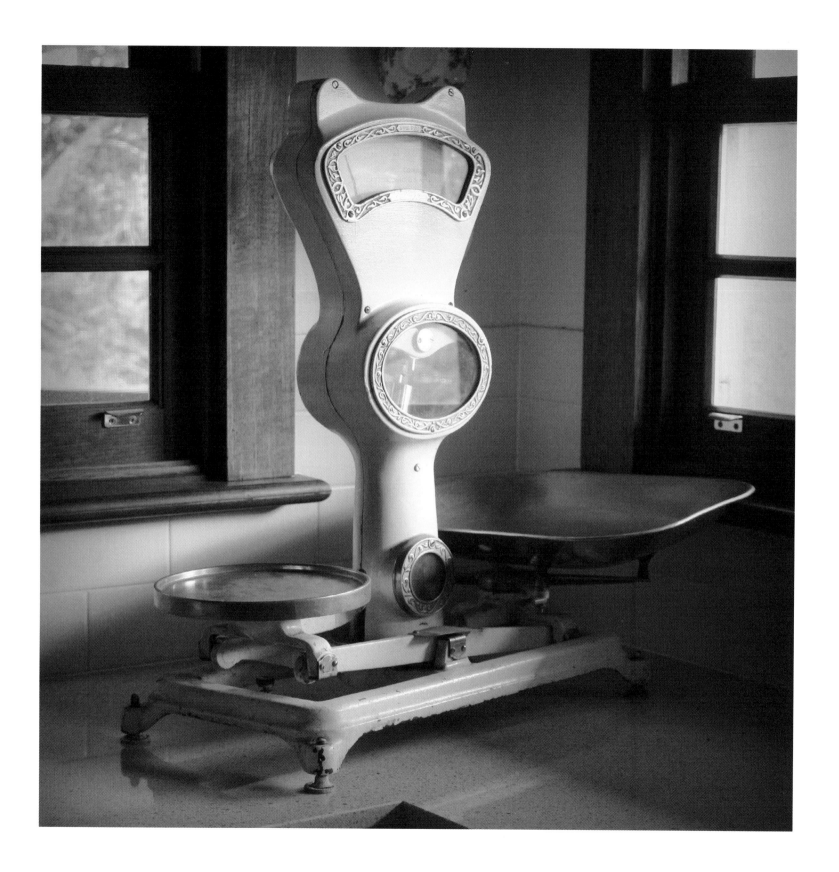

Living Room Design

Country living rooms are a pleasure to design. If planned correctly, they can be filled with a rich variety of design elements, including classic architectural detailing, elegant furnishings and whimsical accessories.

I often begin the process with an open fire as a focal point. A large open fireplace with handcrafted detailing and antique furniture clustered around it is typical of a country living room. A beautifully upholstered sofa, an old throw draped over a traditional wooden chair and appropriately placed side tables and ottomans create a casual and comfortable elegance. To make each piece unique – as if the collection came together over time without planning – I use common things in uncommon ways, so that they are practical and enticing. My favourite things include stacking two or three vintage suitcases to create a side table; suitcases can double as storage for things that are not often used. I have used old wooden boxes as coffee tables, kitchen dressers as bookshelves and antique wooden rowing oars to hang curtains.

Well-crafted vintage wood tables, chairs and cabinetry are all part of country design. To choose pieces that have a worn appeal to them and that are sturdy enough for everyday use, is the aim. A dent or a scratch in a table or cabinet is not a bad thing – it will add to its character and appeal. I try to keep wood tones within the same tonal range, but add an element of eclectic flair by not matching them exactly.

The use of fabrics and upholstery in muted natural tones is prevalent, yet rarely used in anything too coordinated. Faded colours work well in a country living room with checks and stripes, adding contrast when required. I prefer using a wide range of textures in varying natural shades for upholstery and soft furnishings. Endeavouring to keep window treatments simple, I use soft clean lines and simple coordinated tiebacks.

Harmony in the room is maintained by grouping items into vignettes.

Accessories are always important: from throw pillows on the furniture to books on the mantle; nearly every surface is a possible display space in a country-style living room. I use vintage prints to fill the walls and old silverware, ceramic vases and antique *objet d'art* grouped on tabletops and shelves. Harmony in the room is maintained by grouping items into vignettes; for example, grouping ornaments of similar colours on a mantle or sideboard and stacking vintage books on a side table with a walking stick or scarf really sets the scene. A living room should be a display of interesting objects and reflect the warmth, comfort and history of country style.

To choose pieces that have a worn appeal to them and that are sturdy enough for everyday use, is the aim.

PERCY JEFFERSON & Co., Pty. Ltd.

TOBACCONISTS Etc.

567, Bourke St., MELBOURNE, C.1.

BRITISH MADE.

Bedroom Design

Decorating a bedroom in 'true' country style allows me to work with an unpretentious, traditional look that dates back centuries. A country-style bedroom harks back to a time when life was simpler and people often made their own home furnishings and decor.

Like the living room, bedrooms do not need furniture in matched sets; in fact it is something that I avoid. I scour antique stores, auction rooms and markets for separate pieces in the right style and often add something unexpected; for example, an old farmhouse door can be converted into a perfect headboard; a restored vintage packing crate can become a perfect bedside table; and an old storage trunk or bench at the foot of the bed can serve as extra storage or seating. Again, I think utilitarian. I might use a small bookcase to hold boots and shoes or a chair or two in a corner with a stack of large coffee table books acting as a side table.

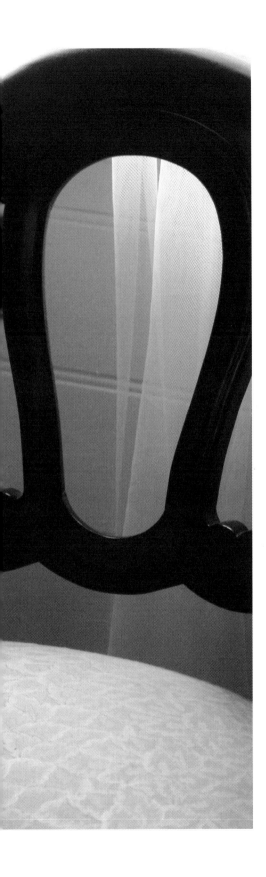

The colours that work for a country bedroom are those that are soft and light. In particular, I find different shades of white are perfect for the base colour, although I sometimes use darker variations, such as beige and cream in place of white. While some accents can include a variety of earthy colours, such as pale tones of blue, green and brown, the overall effect of the colours should be light and airy. At the turn of the 20th century, wallpaper was

a luxury in a country home. This fact encourages me to reintroduce it occasionally in a bedroom in either a very muted shade or a neutral background with a subtle detailed pattern.

The furniture that best fits a country bedroom is typically made from wood and should, at least, look as though it may have been handmade; this style often features wooden beds, dressers and nightstands with rough-looking or antique edges.

Bedding is one of the most important elements in creating a country look for a bedroom. Types of bedding that complement the style can be a handmade quilt or a fluffy down comforter. If I am looking to add a truly original feel to a bedroom, I use antique linen sheets on the bed, rather than newer cotton versions.

A country-style

harks back to a

bedroom time when life was simpler.

Bedding is one of the most important elements in creating a country look for a bedroom.

Bathroom Design

Designing a country bathroom is one of my favourite projects. I aim at achieving a plain yet sophisticated finish with an aged white colour scheme and classic fittings.

Of course, I need to decide how 'original' I am going to take the design of a bathroom; while I prefer using vintage pieces wherever possible, I must sometimes consider the use of modern reproductions as well.

My favourite pieces in a bathroom are a vintage pedestal sink; an antique dresser, at sometime in its life, converted into a vanity for a basin and counter top; and the strongest image that comes to mind when designing a country style bathroom, an old clawfoot bathtub. I give any modern elements an older look and feel, or at least distract from them with such effects as white-washing vanities and replacing bench tops, dispensing with contemporary chrome medicine cabinets and replacing them with original cupboards and hanging vintage mirrors in antique frames.

If I can, I pare back a room and create a fresh shell with classic white tiling and lining board. I then add original elements, such as cabinetry with vintage fittings and antique handles, goose-neck taps with porcelain details and antique light fixtures. Freestanding furniture, such as a dresser or chest of drawers are great options and can also serve as extra storage. Flooring is best in a natural material like wood or handmade tile.

It is often the small decisions made in country design that make the room, especially a bathroom because of its size, from adding a rustic-looking clothes basket, to an antique soap holder because authenticity again, is key! In a country bathroom it is these finishing touches that set off the design as a whole.

I need to decide how 'original' I am going to take the design of a bathroom; I prefer using vintage pieces wherever possible

the strongest image
to mind when designing a
style bathroom, an old claw-

that comes

country

foot tub.

Conclusion

'Country' as I have described it in this book, has and always will have an enormous place in my life.

As a child, I dreamt of witnessing my ancestors' country life firsthand, embracing their simpler ways and their seemingly quieter and more graceful existence.

Looking back, the style that I have described is very much a part of who I am and what I do. I am lucky to have had an upbringing surrounded by it. To be able to continue living amongst it now, in my adult life, I consider a blessing.

I treasure the sentimental connection I have with it, from my deeply engrained family influences, to my work as a designer in more recent years. It has quite an emotional hold on me and I cherish the feelings it conveys.

It is a classic yet unpretentious style and I will forever be bound by its graceful charm.